Classroom Strategies

Classroom Strategies

A Tool Kit for Teaching English Language Learners

Barbara Muchisky

Teacher Ideas Press

An imprint of Libraries Unlimited
Westport, Connecticut • London

Library of Congress Cataloging-in-Publication Data

Muchisky, Barbara, 1943–
  Classroom strategies : a tool kit for teaching English language learners / Barbara Muchisky.
    p. cm.
  Includes bibliographical references and index.
  ISBN 978-1-59158-485-8 (alk. paper)
  1. English language—Study and teaching—Foreign speakers. I. Title.
PE1128.A2.M83 2007
  428.2'4—dc22   2007013341

British Library Cataloguing in Publication Data is available.

Library of Congress Catalog Card Number: 2007013341
ISBN: 978-1-59158-485-8

First published in 2007

Libraries Unlimited/Teacher Ideas Press, 88 Post Road West, Westport, CT 06881
A Member of the Greenwood Publishing Group, Inc.
www.lu.com

Printed in the United States of America

The paper used in this book complies with the
Permanent Paper Standard issued by the National
Information Standards Organization (Z39.48–1984).

10   9   8   7   6   5   4   3   2   1

Contents

Acknowledgments

I am grateful to Lincoln, Nebraska educators Deborah Levitov, Judy Beste, and Billie Meyer for their advice and encouragement. Andrew Lutes provided much-needed technical assistance and designed the original graphics in this text. Dennis Muchisky of Central Missouri University graciously checked the accuracy of linguistic terminology. Clip art images are from Clipart.com.

Introduction

The field of English language teaching has gained attention in the last twenty years as our schools welcome and educate greater numbers of young students whose primary language (or sometimes languages) is one other than English. Some students are recent arrivals from another country who have had little or no exposure to English. Others have lived in the United States for some time while mostly speaking another language at home. As a result, English language learners are a diverse group, representing many languages, cultures, abilities, and experiences. The services these students receive are likewise varied. Some school systems have developed highly structured programs over the years that prepare and support ELL students as they gradually acquire English language proficiency in speaking, listening, reading, and writing. Other schools are just beginning to cope with a population of nonnative speakers. They may be in the early stages of developing a plan to deliver services to a growing number of students.

Today's English language teachers are increasingly well-trained and knowledgeable about language acquisition theory and practice. However, many who are new to language teaching express doubts about how to deliver and organize the content they teach into practical and accessible lessons. This book offers strategies collected over the years that form a toolkit of activity templates for the delivery of many kinds of content. Just as the home toolkit contains basic tools that serve many functions, these activity templates provide teachers with a repertoire of practical ideas which can be recycled and reused. They are intended to supplement a comprehensive language teaching program.

Young children respond to the familiar. Routines in school are reassuring and comforting. Imagine how much more so this applies to students coming from another language and culture. An activity that has a familiar outline is much easier to understand than one that is completely new. An effective language teaching activity provides an expected, predictable format showcasing content that is just a little bit new. An easily understood activity will allow the content to take center stage.

New content-related materials are being published every year that are very appropriate developmentally and culturally. However, before the advent of colorful books, posters, CDs, and teachers' guides, many English language teachers scrambled day-to-day to create lessons out of ideas borrowed from others or invented in desperation! Many of those ideas have remained part of the routines and repertoires that serve us well today.

The suggestions presented in this book include a description of each activity template or framework, content variations, and extensions for independent learning. In addition, several sample lessons are included that demonstrate how a template can be adapted to teach specific content. Many of the lessons are followed by reproducible pages for general or content-specific use.

Chapter One speaks to the importance of routines in creating a manageable plan for teaching English language learners. Routines are crucial for students and teachers alike. They help students feel comfortable and confident, while giving teachers a predictable framework for planning lessons and presenting content.

Chapter Two features activities for the practice and review of content vocabulary. The key to acquiring new vocabulary for native language speakers and second language learners alike is repeated exposure over time to new words and phrases in a meaningful and comprehensible context. These exercises are intended to motivate young students to engage in repeated practice while maintaining enthusiasm for learning.

Chapter Three offers several activities for spelling practice. The direct teaching of spelling may be included in the ELL curriculum as an intrigal part of reading instruction or as a part of thematic instructional units. Students experience a routine that is a regular feature of the elementary classroom. They are introduced to the notion of studying lists of spelling words at school and at home.

Chapter Four focuses on reading instruction. Students who are literate in another language will transfer these skills to English. Others who have not been exposed to the reading process in their first language will be learning to read at the same time they are learning the English language. Reading comprehension for second language learners requires a formidable understanding of vocabulary, syntax, and usage.

Chapter Five addresses writing, possibly the most challenging of the four domains of English language learning. Children do not practice this academic skill incidentally for the most part. Progress in speaking, listening, and even reading, does not necessarily transfer to good communicative writing. Direct instruction and frequent opportunity for practice are essential for students who will be judged throughout their school experience on the quality of their writing.

The activity templates presented in this book are intended to supplement a comprehensive ELL program that addresses all aspects of language learning. A toolkit of familiar, easily understood activities allows teachers to promote the amount of repeated practice necessary for students to learn new linguistic and academic content.

Chapter One

Routines

Although routines are a feature of every classroom, they are especially important for English language learners. Routines represent the familiar, the expected, the comfortable. Imagine how many new experiences our students face every day. By establishing a set of routines, we can create a secure environment that allows all learners to participate at their own comfort levels. Within each routine are opportunities for both newcomers and more advanced language learners to express themselves. The activities set forth in this chapter are already familiar to elementary school teachers. The variations and extensions of each activity are intended to demonstrate how a simple lesson template can be expanded to suit many language teaching situations.

The routines a teacher selects for her classroom depend, of course, on the age and English proficiency of students, as well as the amount of time allotted each day for ELL instruction. The templates in this chapter can be adapted for a variety of students and purposes. The **Daily Calendar** and **Monthly Calendar** are most appropriate for beginning-level students. These activities expose students to temporal concepts and math vocabulary that can be quite abstract. The calendar provides a visual support for teaching this language.

Other activities presented in this chapter are easily adaptable for any age or level of English in elementary school. The **Daily Message** gives students a road map for the day's lessons and introduces or reviews key vocabulary. The **Word of the Day** also provides a means of reviewing vocabulary that relates to thematic content. This activity might be used effectively to align ELL instruction with the curriculum being taught in the regular education classroom. **Follow Directions** is a brief exercise that prepares students to become more independent in all classroom settings. Often our students expect and wait for a verbal prompt from the teacher for every assignment. The **Monthly Memory Book** can be included in a comprehensive writing program in the ELL classroom and provides a record of writing growth throughout the school year.

Routines are good for teachers too. These activities can be adjusted and inserted into the curriculum with minimal planning and preparation. By inserting new content into established routines, we have more time for attention to individual student needs.

Daily Calendar

Number of Participants: Unlimited
Materials Needed:

- Large calendar on pocket chart or bulletin board

- Cards labeled with words for each of the 12 months and 7 days

- Cards with numbers up to 31 to represent dates

- Cards labeled with the words "yesterday," "today," and "tomorrow"

- Labeled pictures depicting seasons and weather conditions

- Three cups or containers and 200 plastic drinking straws

- Shapes for number line that can be placed around the room

- Real or toy coins (five pennies, two nickels, two dimes, two quarters, a half dollar)

- Real or toy dollar bill

Note: Many calendar items are available commercially. Teacher-created materials (cards, labeled pictures, shapes) should be large enough to be easily viewed by all students in the classroom.

Call on students individually to respond verbally to questions about the month, day, and date as they manipulate the cards to set the daily calendar correctly. Students also use cards to label the temporal concepts: yesterday (past tense), today (present tense), and tomorrow (future tense). Students can also identify the current season and weather conditions by selecting an appropriate picture to display with the daily calendar.

Create and maintain a record of the number of days that school has been in session since the beginning of the academic year by adding one straw each day to "place value" cups or containers. These containers are labeled "ones," "tens," and "hundreds." When ten straws have accumulated in the "ones" container, a student can bundle them together with a rubber band and place the bundle in the "tens" container. Likewise, when ten bundles are collected in the "tens" container, they can be bundled altogether again and placed in the "hundreds" container. It will be easy to review how many hundreds, tens, and ones make up the "number of the day."

The same concept of place value can be demonstrated each day by adding a penny each new day, then regrouping the pennies into, nickels, dimes, quarter, half dollars, and dollar. Continue adding to this amount (which should be displayed in a line from right to left) each day of the school year. This will also provide practice in naming and learning the value of coins and a dollar.

The class "number line" is prominently displayed (most effectively in linear fashion) in the classroom. Various shapes represent ones, fives, and tens. (Sample shapes follow this activity.) A student writes the "number of the day" on the shape and adds it to the number line. This number line can then be used for counting (forward and backward), skip counting, distinguishing odd and even numbers, practicing ordinal numbers, performing computation operations, and reviewing ordering concepts (before, after, between, next, and so on).

Variations

- As they become more proficient in speaking, students may be selected to play the role of teacher in asking the questions about the calendar items and prompting others to complete the daily calendar routine.

- The questions and prompts usually given by the teacher can be written on sentence strips and presented to students (in the usual or mixed order) in written instead of verbal form.

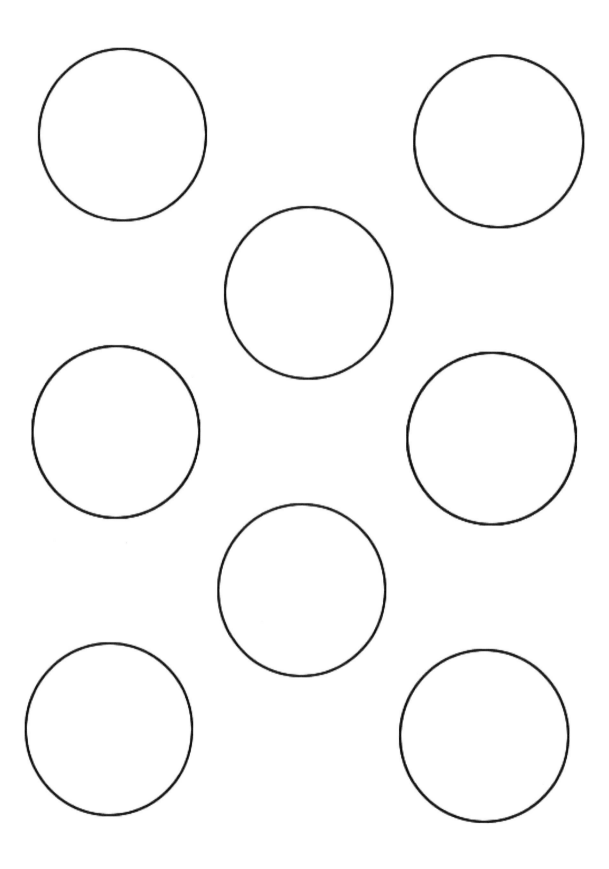

Monthly Calendar

Number of Participants: Unlimited
Materials Needed:

- Copy of generic monthly calendar for each student

- Transparency of generic monthly calendar

On the first school day of every month, distribute a generic monthly calendar to each student. (A sample generic calendar follows this activity.) Using an overhead transparency as a model, fill in the month, days, and dates, encouraging student input. Students complete their individual calendars in like fashion. After the calendars are complete, identify anticipated events and activities, writing them in the appropriate calendar spaces. Include holidays, school vacations, birthdays, field trips, assemblies, and other special events.

This activity presents an opportunity each month to review sequencing vocabulary: before, after, next, after that, then, and between. Students also gain more practice with ordinal numbers.

Variations

- When students become more familiar with this activity, they can take turns entering numbers or words on the transparency.

- Younger children can illustrate their calendars to represent the season, weather, or activities anticipated in the month.

- Use the calendar to create word problems: "What date is the third Monday of the month?" "How many Sundays are in this month?" "What date comes between the 12th and the 14th of the month?" and so on.

Extensions

- Calendars can be taken home to help families anticipate school events. A small piece of magnet (cut from a roll) can be affixed to the back of the paper, and the calendar can be attached to the refrigerator at home.

- Save or reproduce calendars to be bound together later as a record of the year's events.

Sun.	Mon.	Tues.	Wed.	Thurs.	Fri.	Sat.

Daily Message

Number of Participants: Unlimited
Materials Needed:

- Chalkboard or marker board

Write a message on the board describing plans for the day (or session). This will introduce or review thematic vocabulary and can target the language level of the class. Read the message aloud, pointing to each word. Next ask students to read the message in unison, or call on one student to read the message. Then select a student each day who will come to the board to be the "eraser." Students at their seats take turns reading any word at random from the message. Some students will actually read a word, and others may only remember a word they have heard. The "eraser" locates that word and erases it. The next student calls out another word to be erased, and so on, until the entire message has been erased.

Variations

- If a student is unable to read any of the remaining words in the message, he or she can spell the word instead.

- Messages for older students can be written in cursive.

- For older, more advanced students who already read well, a daily schedule can be posted. Then, when a particular activity has been completed, that item can be erased, checked off, or crossed out.

- Relevant phonemic, semantic, or syntactic elements can be highlighted or brought to the attention of students before erasing begins.

Sample Messages

Beginning Level

Good Morning Students:

Today we will talk about butterflies. After lunch we will learn about shapes.

Ms. M.

Intermediate Level

Hello Students:

This a.m., we'll study the life cycle of a butterfly, from an egg to a caterpillar, to a chrysalis, to an adult. In the p.m., we'll measure around squares, rectangles, triangles, and hexagons.

Ms. M.

Advanced, Older Students

Schedule for Today:

a.m.

- *Read chapter on metamorphosis of a butterfly*
- *Discuss stages of development from embryo to adult*

p.m.

- *Solve problems related to the perimeter of geometric shapes.*

Word of the Day

Number of Participants: Unlimited

Materials Needed:

- Pocket chart calendar or wall calendar (optional)

- Words printed on cards that fit into calendar spaces (optional)

- Chalkboard or whiteboard (optional)

Display a new word each day. (Sample word lists follow this activity.) This can be a word related to the month or season , or it can be a word related to the theme or topic the students are currently studying. The word can be displayed in the pocket chart calendar or on a wall calendar, or it can simply be written on the board. This activity can take a short time or a more extended time each day, depending on the variations appropriate for the particular grade or language level of the students.

Variations

- Use these words to create spelling lists or add to current spelling lists as extra credit words.

- Ask students to say or write original sentences including the target word.

- Dictate a sentence containing the word of the day. Use word wall words for the rest of the words in the sentence. These sentences can be written in a booklet or notebook for reading practice. Students can read the previous day's sentence before writing the new one.

- Use the word to highlight a particular phonemic or semantic element. Brainstorm other words that contain that same element. For example, if the word of the day is "week," students might think of "seek," "cheek," or "sleek."

- Younger or beginning students can illustrate the word on a dry erase board, on paper, or in a notebook.

- The word of the day can be entered into a student dictionary. Students with good first language literacy can add a translation of the word in their own languages.

Extensions

- At an end of a month, remove all word of the day cards to an envelope. Put at a independent learning center for alphabetizing practice. For younger children or beginning students, place only words with different initial letters in the envelope.

- At an independent learning center, set up a sorting activity using the word cards from a given month. For example, students could sort by first letter, by number of syllables, by category, and so on. This is a good activity for partners.

SEPTEMBER

school	ruler	glue
teacher	lunch	paper
student	recess	pencil
computer	chalk	desk
eraser	board	crayon
notebook	marker	book
season	fall	autumn
classroom	scissors	backpack

OCTOBER

leaves	trees	change
cool	weather	colors
library	gym	principal
playground	office	sweater
jacket	apple	pumpkin
Halloween	carve	costume
trick or treat	mask	please
thank you	bag	candy

NOVEMBER

read	write	draw
spell	play	work
alphabet	study	learn
cold	foggy	gloves
sweat shirt	jeans	football
harvest	family	travel
Thanksgiving	turkey	meal
grateful	pie	bake

DECEMBER

winter	inside	scarf
boots	mittens	pajamas
socks	jacket	friends
celebrate	holiday	cookies
Christmas	present	gift
Hanukkah	Kwanza	card
stamp	letter	store
shopping	house	home

JANUARY

Ramadan	New Year	snow
freezing	flurries	ice
blizzard	snowman	sled
skates	build	hill
basketball	art	music
homework	math	add
subtract	multiply	divide
number	count	facts

FEBRUARY

ground hog	calendar	year
month	week	day
date	valentine	heart
friendship	poem	red
love	flower	mail
father	mother	sister
brother	grandma	grandpa
cousin	aunt	uncle

MARCH

spring	cloudy	windy
kite	sky	fly
St. Patrick	green	pinch
report card	field trip	test
clock	time	hour
minute	second	money
dollar	half-dollar	quarter
dime	nickel	penny

APRIL

April fool	**joke**	**rainy**
raincoat	**hail**	**tornado**
drizzle	**lightning**	**thunder**
umbrella	**grow**	**grass**
seeds	**plant**	**stem**
roots	**leaf**	**blossom**
soil	**sun**	**water**
dandelion	**tulip**	**rose**

MAY

outside	shorts	sandals
T-shirt	jump rope	bicycle
sunglasses	baseball	park
skateboard	soccer	rabbit
bird	egg	nest
Mother's Day	warm	breezy
temperature	ice cream	hot dog
Memorial Day	summer	vacation

Follow Directions

Number of Participants: Unlimited
Materials Needed:

- Directions written on slips of paper, one per student (optional)

- Chalkboard or whiteboard (optional)

- Paper or notebook for each student

Prepare students for this activity by reviewing vocabulary they will encounter in the written directions: **write, draw, list, color, circle, cross out, count, add, next to, under, above, top, bottom, middle, left, right,** and so on. Each day, every few days, or once a week, provide students with a written direction that has one, two, or three steps. (Sample directions follow this activity.) The directions can be given on slips of paper or just written on the board. Do not read the directions aloud. Students complete the tasks as directed on a piece of paper or in a notebook. Beginning students can be given simple, one-step directions. As they advance in language and reading proficiency, they can move on to two- and three-step directions.

Variations

- Create a listening activity by giving direction in verbal instead of written form.

- For younger children, give more drawing tasks and fewer writing tasks.

- Use as the first activity of the day or session. When students enter the room, the written directions are on their desks or on the board so that they can begin without further instruction from the teacher.

- When all students are finished, compare papers to see how the task was completed by each student.

- Write directions that contain vocabulary related to a theme or topic you are teaching.

Extension

- When students are familiar with this activity, it can be completed in a center with minimal intervention on the part of the teacher. Designate a place where students put their paper or notebook when finished.

Sample Directions

One-Step Directions:

Write your last name.
Write the numbers from 1 to 10.
Write the alphabet.
Write the seven days of the week.
Write the date today.
Draw your favorite animal.
Draw your school.
Draw your best friend.
Draw your family.
Draw a rainbow.

Two-Step Directions:

Write your birthday. Circle the month.
Write the alphabet. Circle the vowels.
List five foods. Cross out two foods.
Draw an apple. Color the apple red.
Draw a moon. Add a star under it.
Draw your teacher. Write her name under the picture.
Write the numbers from 1 to 20. Circle the even numbers.
Draw a tree. Add a bird in the tree.

Three-Step Directions:

Draw a lake. Add a sailboat in the middle. Write your name next to the picture.

List five words that start with the letter "b." Add your name on top of the page and circle it.

Draw a flower garden. Color the sky blue, and add a yellow sun above the flowers.

List foods you like. Count the number of words in your list. Write the number under the list.

Draw your house in the middle of the page. Add a dog on the bottom of the page. Color the dog brown.

Monthly Memory Book

Number of participants: Unlimited

Materials Needed:

- A copy of a memory book for each student. (A sample memory book follows this activity.) The books can be stapled or bound with plastic binding combs.

- Chalkboard or whiteboard

- Student dictionaries (optional)

This activity gives students practice writing sentences or paragraphs in the personal narrative style. It provides a record of writing progress over the span of a school year. The Memory Book is appropriate for any level of language learner, from newcomer to advanced student. On the last school day of every month, brainstorm with students to recall special things that occurred during that month (field trips, birthdays, projects, etc.) at school or at home. Web these ideas on the board. Spend a few moments practicing how these words or phrases on the web can be changed into complete sentences. Ask students to write as many sentences as possible in their memory books. Newcomer students can write patterned sentences, while advanced students can be expected to demonstrate higher-level writing skills. An additional lined page at the end of this activity can be used to give older students more space to write.

Variations

- Students write a rough draft, then edit and rewrite the entry in the Memory Book.
- Students read their entries to a partner or present it to the entire class for feedback.
- Provide a page for friends and teachers to autograph at the end of the year.

Memory Book

Author: _____

In September I remember

_____

_____

_____

_____

_____

_____

_____

_____

_____

_____

_____

_____

In October I remember

_____

_____

_____

_____

_____

_____

_____

_____

_____

_____

_____

_____

_____

_____

In November I remember

_____

_____

_____

_____

_____

_____

_____

_____

_____

_____

_____

_____

In December I remember

_____

_____

_____

_____

_____

_____

_____

_____

_____

_____

_____

_____

In January I remember

_____

_____

_____

_____

_____

_____

_____

_____

_____

_____

_____

_____

In February I remember

_____

_____

_____

_____

_____

_____

_____

_____

_____

_____

_____

_____

In March I remember

_____

_____

_____

_____

_____

_____

_____

_____

_____

_____

_____

_____

In April I remember

_____

_____

_____

_____

_____

_____

_____

_____

_____

_____

_____

_____

In May I remember

_____

_____

_____

_____

_____

_____

_____

_____

_____

_____

_____

Chapter Two

Content Vocabulary

Teaching content vocabulary is at the heart of any program designed for English language learners. From the beginner who is mastering just enough survival vocabulary to get started in an English-speaking environment to the advanced learner who is approaching native-like fluency, the task of acquiring new vocabulary is never ending. Indeed, even speakers of English as a first language must spend a lifetime adding to their own lexical repertoires. A key element for anyone acquiring vocabulary is exposure and repetition over time in multiple, meaningful contexts. A thematic approach to language instruction provides context-rich lessons in which sets of vocabulary words are taught and practiced. Students encounter these English words over and over throughout the unit or theme they are studying. The activity templates in this chapter are meant to provide practice with vocabulary that has been introduced within this type of context. For elementary-aged children, exposure and repetition must involve *variety*. The same content vocabulary can be practiced in many ways. Students will be motivated by the game-like nature of an activity; however, the teacher's objective of teaching content vocabulary can be achieved at the same time.

The first three activities in this chapter, **Around the World, Memory, and Go Fish,** are staples of the elementary classroom. They are quickly learned by students, require little in the way of materials, and can be improvised quickly as the situation demands.

OOPS is another activity that students can play over and over with different content vocabulary while remaining motivated and engaged. Remarkably, children do not seem to tire of these games.

Activities that lend themselves to group instruction do not have to involve elaborate materials or excessive preparation time. Many teachers will already have the necessary picture or word cards that can be adapted for these activities. **What's Missing**, **Pictionary,** and **Who Am I?** can all be played with visual materials that may already be part of a given instructional unit. **Name Something** can be tailored to fit a particular theme or used generically as a quick activity to fill a few minutes of extra time.

Young students need to move. Indeed, tactile and kinesthetic experiences enhance language learning. Some of the activities in this chapter promote movement. To play **What's in the Bag?** students reach into a bag to identify objects with only the sense of touch. **Scavenger Hunt** and **Line Up** all allow students to move about with a purpose. Students interact with classmates as they move in **Find Your Partner** and **Work the Room.**

Around the World

Number of Participants: Five to twelve
Materials Needed:

- Picture, letter, or word cards

This versatile activity is well known to elementary teachers. Students sit in a circle at a table or on the floor. Choose a student to begin and ask him to stand behind another student. Those two students will be the first players. Show a card to the two players. The first player to identify the card wins that round and moves on to stand behind the next player. (The player who loses sits down in the vacant spot.) The next card is revealed to the players and, again, the winning player is the student who is first to call out the item. Play continues. If one student goes "around the world" or completes the circle without sitting down, he will take on the role of teacher.

Variations

The variations of this activity are limitless. For example, students can practice:

- Uppercase and lowercase letters

- Sight words

- Thematic vocabulary words

- Math computation facts

- Antonyms*

- Present- and past-tense verbs*

- Contractions*

*Note: To make this activity more challenging, have students respond to the picture or word prompt with a matching word: (big = little; go = went; don't = do not).

Memory

Number of Participants: Two to six
Materials Needed:

- Word and/or picture cards
- Pocket chart (optional)

This activity is most effectively used to practice and review newly learned English vocabulary or structures. To prepare students to play Memory with a small group or partner, set up the word and/or picture cards on a pocket chart or display them on the table or floor. Place one card faceup and the matching card facedown. Call on students to predict the matching card. Turn over to reveal the second card. Continue in this manner until the group has seen all the matching pairs. Mix the cards and spread them randomly facedown on the table or floor. Students work in pairs or small groups to play the game. Each player turns over two cards, saying the word or naming the picture on the card. If the cards match, the player keeps both cards. If the cards do not match, they are replaced facedown in the same position. Play continues until all cards have been matched. Players count cards to determine the winner. Play again with the same or a new set of cards. The number of memory cards in a set for any one game should be manageable for the age and language level of the players.

Variations

- Beginning and younger students may prefer to play with picture cards only. They match two cards, naming each picture as they turn over the card. The pictures can display the same item, opposite items, or related items. This gives students a lot of opportunity for aural/oral practice.

- Students can be directed to use each word in a sentence (statement or question) as they turn over a card.

- Students can match pictures, letters, words, phrases, and even sentences that are related in some way. For example:

    - Uppercase and lowercase letters (N-n)
    - Cardinal and ordinal numbers (three-third)
    - Matching phonemic elements (bat-cat; hot-not)
    - Thematic vocabulary items (train-train)
    - Synonyms (happy-glad)
    - Antonyms (over-under)
    - Contractions (can't-can not)
    - Verb tenses (play-played; go-went)
    - Idioms (it's raining cats and dogs-it's raining a lot)

Extensions

- When students can play without direct supervision, this makes a good independent learning center activity.

- Use picture and word cards to play **Around the World**. A group of beginning or younger students can simply identify the picture or word cards as they play the game. A more advanced group of students can identify the matching words.

Sample Lesson: Memory

Level: Intermediate
Objective: To practice irregular past-tense verbs in isolation and/or in sentences.
Directions: Complete some or all of the following activities.

Part One

1) Place matching pairs of irregular verbs on pocket chart, table, or floor. (Sample irregular verb pairs follow this activity.) Turn the present-tense verb faceup and the past-tense verb facedown. 2) Call on students in turn to read the first verb and try to recall the matching past tense form. You may need to prompt students by using sentence frames: "I usually drink milk for breakfast." "Yesterday I ...." 3) Remove the past-tense verbs and mix them together. Pass out one or more cards in random order to students. 4) Call on students to match the past-tense verbs they are holding to the matching present tense verb.

Part Two

1) Pass out sets of matching cards to pairs or small groups of students. The size of the set should be appropriate to the age and proficiency level of the students. 2) Tell students to place the cards in random order facedown on the table or floor. 3) The first student turns any two cards faceup, reading each out loud. If a student cannot read the words, other students or the teacher prompt her. 4) If the pair is not a match, both cards are returned to the same spot, facedown. If the pair is a match, the student keeps her two cards. 5) Play continues until all pairs are matched. The winner is the student who has the most cards. 6) Students can play again with the same set or new set of cards.

Part Three

1) Play as above. 2) When a student makes a match, she composes a pair of sentences with the two verbs. To help students with this temporal concept, ask them to use the word "usually" in a present-tense sentence and words such as "yesterday," "last week," or "last year" in the past-tense sentence. This activity works better with adult supervision.

IRREGULAR VERB PAIRS

begin	began
break	broke
bring	brought
buy	bought
do	did
drink	drank
eat	ate
find	found
go	went
get	got
give	got
hear	heard

hide	hid
hold	held
keep	kept
know	knew
make	made
ride	rode
run	ran
say	said
sing	sang
take	took
think	thought
write	wrote

Go Fish

Number of Participants: Three to six
Materials Needed:

- Picture cards (sets of four duplicate cards make up the deck)

- Pocket chart (optional)

This well-known activity allows students to review and practice previously learned vocabulary. Before beginning to play with a given set of picture cards for the first time, display a picture from each set on the pocket chart, table, or floor. Ask students to identify each picture in the deck. Practice the phrase, "Do you have a …?" when naming each item. To play, mix the cards and deal five cards to each student. Put the remaining cards in the center of the group (the fish pond). The first player begins by calling on any other student in the group and asking, "Do you have a …?" If that student has one or more cards with the given picture, he must give them up to the player who requested them. If he does not have any of the cards requested, he says, "Go fish!" and the first student draws a card from the fish pond. Play continues in this fashion. When a student completes a set of four duplicate cards, he lays the set down in front of him. Play resumes until all sets have been laid on the table. The child with the most cards on the table is the winner.

Variations

- Older students can play with sets of word cards instead of picture cards.

- A deck with sets of action pictures can be used with different lead sentences: "Do you like to (ride a bike?) If the student who is called on has an action picture of riding a bike, he can reply, "Yes, I do," as he hands over the card(s) or "No, I don't. Go fish."

- This activity is an effective way for students to practice a wide range of vocabulary words and concepts, including:

  – Letters of the alphabet

  – Numbers

  – Colors

  – Shapes (geometric and solid)

  – Thematic vocabulary (animals, food, clothing, etc.)

Extensions

- Remove two cards from each picture set and use them to play **Memory**.

- Mix picture cards from various thematic vocabulary sets together and ask students to sort them into categories. This is a good independent learning center activity.

- Write the words for the pictures on a lotto-style sheet. Ask students to place each picture card on the corresponding word square.

Sample Lesson: Go Shopping

Level: Beginner

Objective: To practice names of classmates, to exchange brief questions and answers, and to review food vocabulary.

Directions:

1) Review food picture cards before beginning to play. (Sample food picture cards follow this activity.) 2) Mix the picture cards and deal five to each player. Place the remaining cards in the middle of the table (the grocery store). 2) The first player calls another player by name and asks, "Do you like (ice cream)?" Students must be holding at least one card of a set to request that food. 3) If the player who is called on has one or more of the cards requested, he replies, "Yes, I do," and relinquishes the card(s). If the player does not hold that card, he responds, "No, I don't. Go shopping!" 4) When a player collects four cards of the same food, he places the set on the table in front of him. 5) Play continues until all sets have been collected. 6) Students count their cards to determine the winner.

Variations

- Practice singular and plural usage: "Do you like (an apple)? "Do you like (grapes)?

- Practice mass and count nouns: "Do you like (a carrot)? "Do you like (corn)?

- Practice use of indefinite pronouns: "Do you like (an orange)? "Do you like (a banana)?

Extensions

Play categories with food cards. Sort pictures into:

- Breakfast, lunch, dinner, snacks

- Food groups

- Foods I like/foods I don't like

- Healthy food/junk food

From *Classroom Strategies: A Tool Kit for Teaching English Language Learners* by Barbara Muchisky.
Westport, CT: Teacher Ideas Press. Copyright © 2007 by Barbara Muchisky.

OOPS

Number of Participants: Two to eight
Materials Needed:

- Word cards

- Coffee can or other container (optional)

Vocabulary words are printed on index cards. The word "OOPS" is written on every fifth or sixth card. Cards are placed inside a coffee can or simply piled facedown on the table or floor. Students take turns drawing cards and reading the word. After reading the word, a player places the card in front of her. Students who cannot read the card drawn are helped by the other players or the teacher. When a player draws an OOPS card, she must give up all her cards and return them to the discard pile. She continues to play on her next turn. When all the cards have been drawn, the student with the most cards remaining is the winner.

Variations

This activity can be easy or challenging, depending on age and language level of the students. Sets of OOPS cards can include:

- Lowercase alphabet

- Uppercase alphabet

- Sight words

- Word families

- Thematic vocabulary words

- Antonyms*

- Contractions*

- Irregular verbs*

- Idioms*

- Synonyms*

- Irregular plurals*

*Note: In these variations, students can be required to read the word they have drawn, and then say a corresponding word or phrase. For example, in Antonym OOPS, if the student draws the word "slow," she reads "slow" and also must say "fast."

Students can be asked to use each word they draw in a sentence (either a statement or a question).

Extension

- OOPS makes a good independent learning center activity for groups of two or three students after they have learned how to play.

Sample Lesson: Idiom OOPS

Level: Intermediate to advanced
Objective: To practice common English idioms and their meanings.
Directions:

1) Ask students to cut apart the sheet of paper on the grid lines and mix up the slips of paper. (Sample idioms and meanings follow this activity.) 2) Two or three students join their piles together. 3) Place the pile facedown in the center of the group or put the papers into an envelope so the student drawing a paper cannot see the words on the paper. 4) The students take turns drawing a slip of paper. If the paper contains an idiom, the student must give its meaning. Likewise, if the phrase represents the meaning of an idiom, the student must say the matching idiom. 5) The students keep each slip of paper in front of them. 6) If a player draws OOPS, she must put all her papers on the discard pile and start over when her next turn comes around. 7) Play continues until all papers have been drawn. The winner is the person who has collected the most slips of paper.

Extensions

- Save idiom pairs for a game of **Memory**.

- Have students draw pictures of the idioms and match the pictures to the idioms. For example, draw a picture of a person with very large eyes and a small abdomen to represent the idiom "My eyes are bigger than my stomach."

IDIOM OOPS

I am in hot water.	I am in trouble.
That is a piece of cake.	That is easy.
It costs an arm and a leg.	It is expensive.
I am all ears.	I am listening carefully.
Bite your tongue!	Don't say that!
I have butterflies in my stomach.	I'm nervous.
Zip your lips.	Be quiet.
Chill out!	Relax!
I got up on the wrong side of bed.	I am in a bad mood.
Hit the books.	Study hard.

Don't let the cat out of the bag.	Don't tell as secret.
Shake a leg.	Hurry up.
Hold your horses.	Wait a minute.
You have a green thumb.	You are good at growing things.
My eyes are bigger than my stomach.	I have more food than I can eat.
It's raining cats and dogs.	It's raining very hard.
O O P S	O O P S
O O P S	O O P S
O O P S	O O P S
O O P S	O O P S

From *Classroom Strategies: A Tool Kit for Teaching English Language Learners* by Barbara Muchisky.
Westport, CT: Teacher Ideas Press. Copyright © 2007 by Barbara Muchisky.

What's Missing?

Number of Participants: Four to eight
Materials Needed:

- Pocket chart (optional)

- Large picture cards

This is an appropriate activity for younger or beginning students. Review the vocabulary items as you place the cards randomly on the pocket chart, table, or floor. Limit the number of cards according to the age and ability of the children. Choose one student to go outside of the room and stand near the door without looking in. Call on another student to name one of the pictures in the display. Remove that picture and place it out of sight. Tell the second student to go to the door and invite the first student back into the room. When she returns, the class calls out, "What's missing?" She tries to name the missing picture from memory. If she does not succeed after a few guesses, ask the class to give her clues (initial letter or sound, color, use, etc.). When the picture has been identified, return it to its space in the display and choose another student to leave the room. Continue until each child has had a turn.

Variation

- Use realia instead of pictures. Spread the items on the table or floor. After reviewing the vocabulary, tell students to close their eyes. Remove one item and tell students to open their eyes again. Call on students to guess what's missing. This works well for practicing the names of objects in the classroom: scissors, glue, ruler, and so on.

Extension

- Place realia on the table or floor, as above. Ask students to look at the display for one minute and try to remember where everything is. Cover the objects with a large cloth or paper. Give students paper and pencil and tell them to draw the items from memory. When they have had a few minutes to do this, remove the covering and compare the original display with their drawings. Work together to label the objects they have drawn.

Pictionary

Number of Participants: Four to ten
Materials Needed:

- Paper or whiteboards

- Word cards

Choose a theme for this activity (food, animals, transportation, etc.). Call on several students to name an item from the category. Make a simple, quick sketch of the item on paper or a board, emphasizing only its most basic characteristics. Tell students that they will be making similar drawings. Divide students into two teams and give each team a large paper or marker board. Arrange the teams so that they are sitting some distance from each other. Call one student from each team to come to where you are seated. Show them both a word card, telling them to read the word but not to say it aloud. If one or both of the children cannot read the word, whisper it to them. Tell the two students to go quickly to their team's paper or marker board and draw a picture of the word they have read. Emphasize that they must not say anything to their team members or they will lose their turn. As soon as the children begin drawing, their teammates call out words that would identify the picture. As soon as someone from either team guesses the correct word, that round has ended, and their team receives a point. Then two more students come to the teacher to see the next word and play continues. The team with the most points wins the game.

Variations

- Play Pictionary without choosing a particular category. For younger children, select words that are not difficult to draw (tree, square, ball). For nonreaders, whisper the word to be drawn. Older students with greater language proficiency can be challenged to draw more difficult and abstract words (Halloween, surprised, sports).

- Use a game board to play Pictionary. Teams move a game marker each time they correctly guess a word.

Extension

- Partners can play Pictionary as an independent learning center activity. Place the word cards facedown in a pile on the table. Students take turns selecting a word card from the pile and drawing a picture of the word on a marker board or on paper for their partners to guess.

Sample Lesson: Animal Pictionary

Level: Beginner to intermediate
Objective: To hear, say, and comprehend many animal names in a short period of time.
Directions:

1) To prepare, cut apart animal word cards and mix them into a pile. (Sample animal word cards follow this activity.) For less proficient students, use the most basic words. Also prepare the game board and provide one game marker for each team. (A sample generic game board follows this activity.) 2) Ask a student to name an animal. Quickly draw that animal on paper or a board, emphasizing its most identifiable elements. 3) Name an animal and tell students to draw it as quickly as possible on paper or a marker board. Give them a time limit. 4) Divide the students into two groups and position the groups on either side of the game board. 5) Give each group a large piece of paper or a marker board. 6) Call one student from each group to come to the front of the room. Show both of them the same word card. If they are not able to read the word, whisper it to them. 7) Tell both students to return quickly to their groups and draw a picture of the animal without saying the name aloud. 8) Tell the other students to begin guessing the animal as soon as they have any idea what it could be. As soon as someone guesses correctly, the round is over. 8) The student whose team has correctly identified her picture moves the game marker forward on the game board. 9) Play continues as the next two students are called to the front to see another word. 10) The winning team is the first to reach the finish line on the game board.

Extensions

- Put the word cards in an independent learning center for alphabetizing.

- Photocopy two sets of word cards for playing **Memory**.

- Use the word cards to play **Around the World**.

ANIMALS

snake	turtle
bird	dog
fish	cat
horse	cow
chicken	pig
sheep	elephant
lion	monkey
zebra	deer
tiger	butterfly
ladybug	penguin
spider	dolphin

camel	alligator
mouse	bear
ant	duck
eagle	squirrel
kangaroo	gorilla
whale	giraffe
bee	seal
lizard	bat
dinosaur	octopus

		lose a turn		

START

move ahead one space

	lose a turn		move back one space	

move back one space

move ahead one space

FINISH

	move back one space	lose a turn		

Who Am I?

Number of Participants: Two to ten
Materials Needed:

- Large picture or word cards

- Clothespin or other fastener

This is another opportunity for students to hear, say, and comprehend newly learned vocabulary items in a game-like setting. Before beginning, review the pictures or words, talking about some basic characteristics (for example, an elephant is very large, has four legs, big ears, a trunk, and can be found in a zoo). Select a student to come to the front of the room and sit with his back to the other students. Choose one of the large picture or word cards and attach it to the back of his shirt (at the collar works well) with a clothes pin or other fastener. Make sure all of the other students have seen the picture or word before turning the student around to face the class. The student asks questions that can only be answered by the group with "yes" or "no." (For example, "Do I have four legs?") The student continues to ask questions until he has guessed the identity of the picture or word. If he is stuck, he asks the class for clues. (For example, someone in the group might say, "You have big ears.") After he has completed his turn, the student can choose the next child to come forward, and play continues until everyone has had a turn.

Variations

- To play with very young children, review the names of all the pictures. Then seat students in a circle and attach a picture card to the back of each one. Select a student and turn him around until everyone has seen who or what he is. Then the student can ask, "Am I (a dog)?" The group responds "yes" or "no." The child continues to ask questions until he guesses his animal identity.

- Another alternative with very young children can be to have the students take turns selecting pictures to attach to the back of the teacher. In this way, the teacher is the one who forms the questions, and students need only reply "yes" or "no."

- Use Who Am I? to practice thematic vocabulary including:

    – Classroom items

    – People and places in school

    – Food

    – Clothing

    – Animals

    – Characters in a story

    – Workers in the community

    – Types of transportation

Sample Lesson: Who Am I in the Community?

Level: Beginner to intermediate
Objective: To hear, say, and comprehend names and duties of people who work in the community.
Directions:

1) Enlarge pictures of community workers as appropriate for the size of the group. (Sample pictures of community workers follow this activity.) 2) Review names for the workers and talk about where they work as well as what they do in the community. 3) Select a student with good verbal skills to begin. Attach a picture to the back of his shirt and turn him around to reveal his identity to the group. 4) Turn him to face the group and tell him to ask questions about his identity that can only be answered by "yes" or "no." For example, the student might ask, "Do I drive a truck?" "Do I help people who are sick?" "Do I fix your teeth?" 5) Students in the group answer only "yes" or "no" until the questioner guesses his identity or until he needs clues to help him be successful. 6) Play continues until all have had a turn.

Extensions

- Make a mini-book of riddles. Reproduce pictures of community workers and staple them together in book form. Place the pictures facing the back of the book. On the "front" side of each picture, write clues to the identity of the worker who is pictured on the "back" side of the page. For example, "I drive a truck." "I bring letters to your house." "Who am I?"

- Use the picture cards to play **Around the World.**

- Reproduce two pictures of each worker. Play **Memory.**

- Reproduce four pictures of each worker. Play **Go Fish.**

From *Classroom Strategies: A Tool Kit for Teaching English Language Learners* by Barbara Muchisky.
Westport, CT: Teacher Ideas Press. Copyright © 2007 by Barbara Muchisky.

Name Something

Number of Participants: Three to ten
Materials Needed:

- Cards or slips of paper with written descriptors

- Paper bag (optional)

- Chalkboard or whiteboard (or overhead projector)

- Student dry-erase boards (optional)

Practice this activity with the group by drawing a card or slip of paper with written descriptors from a bag or just from a pile on the table. (Sample descriptors follow this activity.) The descriptors tell students to "name something (round)" or "name something (cold)" "name something (used in the kitchen)." Tailor the descriptors to the age and language proficiency of the students. Descriptors can also reflect a current thematic unit of study. For example, "name something (you can wear in the snow)" or "name something (you can wear on your feet)." Call on each student to name something that matches the descriptor. After students have been introduced to this activity and have heard some examples, mix the descriptors in a paper bag. Have students draw a card or paper from the bag, read it aloud, and name something that fits the descriptor. Continue until all children have had several turns.

Variation

- Give each student a small dry-erase board (or small chalkboard). Display the descriptor on the board or overhead projector. Give students a minute to write their own matching word on their individual board. At a signal from the teacher, the students all show what they have written.

Extensions

- Photocopy a list of descriptors to place in an independent learning center. Students work independently or with a partner to write as many nouns as possible to fit each descriptor.

- Teachers like to dismiss students in an orderly way. The teacher can ask individual students to name something before receiving permission to leave the room.

NAME SOMETHING

Name something red.

- -

Name something square.

- -

Name something green.

- -

Name something cold.

- -

Name something round.

- -

Name something flat.

- -

Name something orange

- -

Name something large.

- -

Name something black.

Name something soft.

- -

Name something beautiful.

- -

Name something alive.

- -

Name something delicious.

- -

Name something expensive.

- -

Name something bright.

- -

Name something straight.

- -

Name something furry.

- -

Name something tiny.

Name something smooth.

Name something easy.

Name something bumpy.

Name something hot.

Name something funny.

Name something in the kitchen.

Name something in the classroom.

Name something in the garden.

Name something in the store.

Name something good to eat.

Name something fun to play.

Name something to ride in.

Name something to wear in winter.

Name something to wear in summer.

What's in the Bag?

Number of Participants: Three to ten
Materials Needed:

- Paper lunch bags

- Realia

Select a number of small items representing target vocabulary. Place each small object in a brown lunch bag. Hold the bag in front of students one at a time, telling them to close their eyes and reach into the bag. They feel the shape of the object and think what it might be. Caution them not to identify the item out loud until all students in the group have had a chance to reach into the bag. At a signal from the teacher, all students call out the name of the object. The teacher continues in this manner with the rest of the bags until all of the objects have been identified.

Variations

- Choose the objects in accordance with thematic vocabulary. Make the activity easy or difficult depending on the English proficiency of the group. Easy items might be school supplies (scissors, glue, eraser). More challenging items might be items found in nature (seashell, pinecone, rock).

- Number the bags and display them in front of the room. After all the items have been identified, challenge the students to remember what is in each numbered bag.

- In random order, name items in the bags. As students hear the name of an object, they write the number of its bag on a dry-erase board. Compare boards to see who has identified the correct bag.

- On a piece of paper, students can write the number of each bag, then try to remember and write the name of the object it contains. If spelling is an issue, write all the vocabulary items on the chalkboard in random order.

Scavenger Hunt

Number of Participants: Four to ten
Materials Needed:

- Paper or plastic bags

- Realia or picture cards

- Lists of items to be found

Place objects (small toys are useful for this activity) or picture cards around the room. Depending on the age of the students, these can be in plain sight or hidden. Make a written list of the items or pictures. Give each student a bag and a list, and tell them to find the items as quickly as possible, put each in the bag, and return to their seats. This activity can be used to practice easy or challenging thematic vocabulary. For example, looking for small plastic animals might be easy, while a search for hidden solid shapes might be difficult. The teacher may want to set a timer to indicate when time is up. Call on students to pull objects or pictures from their bags, naming each one as they do so.

Variations

- Assign partners. Give one partner the bag and the other the list. Tell them to work together to find items quickly.

- To make the activity more difficult, give each student or each pair a different list of objects or pictures.

- Move the scavenger hunt outside.

- Do a scavenger hunt in the school library. Give students a list of book titles to find and collect.

- Instead of writing a list of words, write sentences describing the objects or pictures to be found. For example, "Find something that has two wheels and a handlebar" (a toy bicycle).

Line Up

Number of Participants: Six to twelve
Materials Needed:

- Picture or word cards

Divide students into two equal lines, facing the teacher. Select picture or word cards to practice. Display a card to the first two students in line who quickly call out the word. The student who is first to respond correctly goes to the back of his own line. The losing student leaves his own line and moves to the back of the winner's line. Play continues with two new students who are now first in the lines. The lines change, becoming longer and shorter as students move from line to line. Play continues until all students are in one line or until the allotted time has run out. The winning team has all (or the greater number) of players.

Variations

Use this activity to practice:

- Uppercase and lowercase letters
- Sight words
- Math computation facts
- Thematic vocabulary words
- Antonyms*
- Contractions*
- Verb tenses*
- Irregular plurals*

*Note: For a greater challenge, when they are shown the prompt card, students call out a matching word. (For example, if they are shown the singular noun "man," they respond with the plural "men.")

Find Your Partner

Number of Participants: Eight to twenty
Materials Needed:

- Picture and word cards

Prepare sets of two picture or word cards that demonstrate a relationship. Distribute cards randomly, giving each student one card. Tell them to find another student who has a card that "goes with" their card and stand next to that person. If there are an odd number of participants, the teacher keeps one card and looks for a "partner" as well. Students move about the room comparing cards with classmates. When two students find they have a pair, they stand together in one spot. Play continues until each student has found a partner. Partners share their set of words with the group.

Variations

Beginning or younger students can find a partner who is holding the same picture or word card as the one they themselves are holding.

Card sets can represent easy or challenging concepts. For example:

- Uppercase and lowercase letters (A-a)
- A picture and a word (picture of a dog-the word "dog")
- Synonyms (smart-intelligent)
- Antonyms (day-night)
- Present and past tense verbs (dive-dove)
- Idioms (relax-chill out)
- Cardinal and ordinal numbers (three-third)
- Words and their definitions (fragile-breaks easily)

Sample Lesson: Find Your Partner

Level: Intermediate
Objective: To recognize words that fit together to form compound words.
Directions:

1) Photocopy and cut apart the compound word pairs. (Sample compound word pairs follow this activity.) 2) Mix all of the words and randomly distribute them, one to each student. 3) Tell students to move around the room and compare words with their classmates. 4) When two people believe they have formed a compound word, they should stand together. Tell students to make sure the two parts of the compound word are arranged in the proper order. 6) Continue until all have found a partner. 7) Ask each pair of students to read their compound word to the group. Each partner will say only the part of the word he or she is holding.

Extensions

- Use the sets of compound words to play **Memory**.

- Mix the words and put them in an independent learning center. Tell students to match the word sets and make a written list of the compound words.

- Challenge students to make a list of compound words they find during their independent reading time.

COMPOUND WORD SETS

back	pack
sun	flower
play	ground
sail	boat
foot	ball
class	room
chalk	board
wrist	watch
news	paper
rain	coat
snow	flake
birth	day

apple	sauce
pea	nut
water	fall
straw	berry
flash	light
sea	shell
friend	ship
fore	head
ear	ring
tooth	paste
down	town
side	walk

Work the Room

Number of Participants: Unlimited
Materials Needed:

- Paper divided into a grid for each student

This is an activity to promote interaction among the students in the class. Choose a topic about which students will be soliciting information or opinions from other members of the group. Decide on a number of possible responses, and create a grid with that number of spaces. For example, a grid for gathering information about which season students prefer would have four spaces. A grid for recording favorite foods could have any number of spaces. Students will be signing their names in the spaces so that there should be room in each space for several signatures. Label the spaces according to the anticipated responses. For example, the spaces in the seasons grid are labeled winter, spring, summer, and fall. Spaces in a grid about favorite foods are labeled according to the foods the teacher or the class has selected ahead of time. Give each student a copy of this grid. Before beginning the activity, practice forming questions and answers related to the topic. Tell students to circulate around the room asking for information or opinions on the topic. As students respond to questions, they sign the appropriate space on the grid as a record of their response. After the activity has ended, call on students to share some of the results.

Variations

- Beginning or younger students can use a grid that has only two spaces, one for "yes" and one for "no." They can then agree or disagree with a question. For example, "Do you like to play soccer?" They sign their names in the "yes" or "no" space.

- More advanced students can label their own spaces, so that every grid may be unique to that individual.

- Instead of having students sign their own names in the appropriate space on the grid, the questioner can write the names of all students on his own grid, asking for spelling, if needed. This provides practice in spelling the names of classmates.

- Challenge students to create a graph that illustrates the results of their questioning.

- Use this activity to gather information and opinions on many topics, including:

    – Likes and dislikes

    – Family information (number of siblings)

    – Favorites (sports, food, seasons, characters in a story, books)

    – Demographic information (country or state of birth, birthdays)

    – Personal information (weight, height, eye and hair color)

Sample Lesson: Work the Room

Level: Beginning
Objective: To ask and answer questions verbally, to read labels on the grids, and to write names in the appropriate spaces.
Directions: Complete one or more of the following activities.

Part One

1) Practice saying and reading the months of the year. Mix names of the months and have students place them in order on the pocket chart (table, floor, or chalkboard ledge). 2) Ask each student the question, "When is your birthday?" Make index cards showing students' birthdays available for those who need them. 3) In pairs, practice asking and answering, "When is your birthday?" and "My birthday is …." 4) Pass out a blank grid with twelve spaces. (A sample birthday grid and a generic "work the room" grid follow this activity.) 5) Place a transparency of the grid on the overhead projector. 6) Ask the students to say the months one at a time in order. 7) As they identify each month, write the month (or its abbreviation) in a space on the transparency. Ask students to copy the month onto the same space on their individual grids. (*Note:* For younger students, have the months already written on their grids.)

Part Two

1) Tell students to write their own names in the space labeled with the month of their own birthdays. 2) Direct them to move around the room, asking every other student, "When is your birthday?" 3) After a student responds, she writes her name in the appropriate space (month) on her classmate's grid. Each student should solicit input from every other student in the class. 4) When students have finished collecting signatures, call them back together to share information. (For example, "Who had a birthday in October?" "What month had the most birthdays?" "What month had no birthdays?")

Part Three

1) Make line graphs (independently or together as a group) depicting the number of birthdays in each month. 2) Write sentences (independently or together as a group) describing the information in the graph. These can be patterned ("We have three birthdays in January." "We have one birthday in February.") or original ("June has more birthdays than December." "Two people were born in September.")

BIRTHDAY GRID

January	February	March
April	May	June
July	August	September
October	November	December

WORK THE ROOM GRID

Chapter Three

Spelling

Spelling is a traditional part of the elementary curriculum; however, it may or may not be included in ELL instruction. Typically, for beginning-level ELL students, a weekly spelling test serves two purposes. Perhaps most important, it introduces them to a routine they will no doubt encounter in the regular education classroom. It also allows the teacher to tailor the spelling list to meet the curricular or instructional needs of the second language learner. Most often, advanced students study spelling in the regular education classroom rather than in an ELL setting.

English language teachers who do make spelling a part of their daily instruction must choose or create a spelling program that meets their students' needs. For example, if spelling instruction is tied to reading, the teacher may decide to select words on the basis of their phonetic characteristics or on the frequency level of sight words. If the objective of the spelling program is tied to thematic vocabulary units, the selection of words could be determined by frequency of occurrence within the unit.

The activity templates in this chapter are meant for practice within the classroom. They are short, easily learned, and can be repeated with any word list. **Spelling Dictation** with the word wall uses spelling as a vehicle for listening and writing practice. The dictation is a strategy that has been a staple of language teaching for a long time. Its value is still recognized as a powerful teaching and assessment tool. **Categories** encourages students to look for similarities and differences in words. The patterns they discover can help them to recall spelling conventions. **Disappearing Spelling** and **Sparkle** are highly motivating group activities when used as planned or impromptu spelling review.

As well as serving an academic purpose, a spelling program provides a good link between school and home. ELL parents are often eager for their children to have homework. They may come from an educational background in which homework played a significant role. It is sometimes difficult for teachers to assign meaningful homework that can be completed independently by ELL learners. A weekly spelling list can be practiced daily at home, and, indeed, success on "Friday's" test is highly dependent on some effort outside of class.

Spelling Dictation

Number of Participants: Unlimited
Materials Needed:

- Paper and pencil

- Word wall

The objective of this dictation is twofold: to practice writing spelling words in meaningful context and to gain familiarity with words on the word wall. Prepare sentences, each containing one spelling word. Make up the remainder of each sentence from words found on the classroom word wall. The words selected for a given word wall have been chosen as important for that classroom. They should be of appropriate difficulty and frequency. Before beginning to dictate sentences, review with students some of the writing conventions they should keep in mind (capitalization, punctuation, and spacing). Read sentences one at a time for students to write. It works well to read the sentence first at normal speed, again (once or twice) at reduced speed, and finally at a normal rate. Students find it helpful to know in advance how many words are in the sentence. This will give them practice with one-to-one correspondence. Repeat sentences as needed before students hand in their papers.

Variations

- Depending on the age and ability of the learners, it may be appropriate to display the spelling word list as well as the word wall. This makes the dictation an opportunity for practice, not a test.

- If students are still becoming familiar with the word wall and are unable to spot a word, the teacher can give a pointer to a volunteer who will go to the word wall to point out the word in question.

- A spelling dictation can be adjusted to the level of the class. Younger or beginning students can write short, patterned sentences. (For example, "I have it.") Older, more proficient learners can handle more complex and varied sentences. (For example, "Does she still have one of those?")

- Students who do not have spelling as part of their ELL instruction can benefit from sentence dictation as part of their writing instruction. Pairing thematic vocabulary with words from the word wall can be part of the regular writing program. An effective strategy may be to dictate one sentence every day and return it the next day with editing marks. Students can edit this sentence from the previous day before the teacher dictates the new sentence.

Extension

- As an independent learning center activity for more advanced students, assign them to write dictation sentences themselves, using their spelling list and the word wall.

Spelling Categories

Number of Participants: Unlimited
Materials Needed:

- Blank grid

- Transparency (optional)

- Chalkboard or whiteboard (optional)

- Pocket chart (optional)

This activity works best with a spelling word list that is phonics-based and in which there are a limited number of phonological elements. For example, a list that contained words with the "long e sound" represented by "ea" (speak), "ee" (feet), and "e_e" (complete) could be divided into a grid with three sections. It will be necessary to teach this activity first with visual support (overhead transparency, pocket chart, chalkboard, or whiteboard). Put a word ("speak") in the first cell of the grid. Then take the next word ("feet") and hold it near the first word. Ask, "Does this word make the 'long e sound' in the same way or in a different way?" When it is agreed that the sound is made with different letters, place that word in the next horizontal cell (not under the first word). Take each word in turn and, with student input, place each word under another word with a similar vowel pattern. When a new pattern is noticed ("complete") , start a new column on the grid. Continue in this manner until all words have been placed in columns with like-vowel patterns. After students are familiar with this activity, it will not be necessary to work as a group. Merely pass out the blank grid and tell students to figure out which of the words on their spelling list "go together" and to fit them into the grid. After they have finished, compare results and ask students to tell why they have placed certain words together.

Example of a completed grid:

speak	feet	complete
meat	street	these
easy	green	here
treat		

Variations

Some possible categories include:

- Vowel patterns

- Blends

- Singular, plural nouns

- Part of speech

- Prefixes or suffixes

Note: Some thematic or content-based word lists may lend themselves to spelling categories. For example, a spelling list of food words might be divided into a grid based on food groups, or a list of animals might be categorized by number of legs.

Disappearing Spelling

Number of Participants: Three to ten
Materials Needed:

- Chalkboard or whiteboard

Write the spelling list on the chalkboard or whiteboard and underline each letter in the words. Call on students one at a time to look at a word and spell it out loud. After a child has finished spelling a word, erase one random letter from the word, leaving the underline in place. Continue through the list of words in this manner. Start at the beginning of the list again. This time the student (whoever is next in turn) will spell the word aloud, verbally filling in the blank left by the erased letter. After he is finished with the word, erase another random letter, again leaving the underline. In the next round, the word will have two blank spaces, and, in the fourth round, the word will have three blank spaces. Continue while interest is high. Before ending the activity, call on students one at a time to come up to the board and write in the missing letters in the words.

Variations

- After students have filled in the missing letters, choose one student to come to the board. He calls on students one at a time to read any (random) word on the list. He then erases that word and calls on another classmate to read another word. He continues in this manner until all words are erased.

- Follow up with a photocopied sheet of paper listing the spelling words with several blank spaces in each word for students to fill in. Students compare work with a partner to check their spelling.

Sparkle

Number of Participants: Five to twelve
Materials Needed:

- Spelling word list

This is a good activity for practicing spelling words *after* students have had a few days to become familiar with the word list. Tell students to stand behind their chairs (or in a circle on the floor). Begin with any student and make sure play always proceeds in the same direction. Say the first word aloud. The student who begins says the first letter; the next student says the second letter, and so on until the word has been completed. At this point, participants call out "Sparkle," and the student who is next in order must sit down. Play continues with the teacher saying another spelling word. The next student in order begins the word, and Sparkle continues in this manner, with the child who is next in order after the completion of a word sitting down. Finally, there will be only two students left standing. The winner will be the one who finishes by saying the last letter of the last word. It may be necessary to play more than one round of Sparkle to practice all of the words.

Variations

- After students become adept at Sparkle, challenge them to play silently. The teacher says the word and the students spell mentally. After determining that the correct number of letters have been spelled silently, the next-in-line sits down.

- More advanced students with a good knowledge of the English sound system can play **Sparkle** to practice phonological elements of words. Instead of saying each letter in the word, the participants say the letters that make up each phoneme. For example, the word "dish" would be spelled by three people, d-i-sh; the word "though" would be spelled by two students, th-ough.

Chapter Four

Reading

English language learners tend to fall into two groups in terms of reading instruction. Those who have not yet (or ever) learned to read in their first language will face the task of mastering the reading process at the same time as they are acquiring a new language. They must be taught to *read* as well as to *read in English*. Imagine the difficulty of assigning sound and meaning to the arbitrary lines, squiggles, and curves on the page. The irregular nature of the relationship between English sounds and the written language makes this an especially challenging task. The second group of students is made up of those who have already learned to read in their first language. They must now transfer these skills to their new language while acquiring a vast new lexicon. This group does not have to learn to *read*; they only need to learn to *read English*.

Several of the activity templates in this chapter are intended to teach and review skills in the acquisition of the reading process. **Sentence Scrambles** gives children practice with English syntax as they assemble sentences in the proper order. **Find It Fast** exposes students to various types of word usage and requires them to scan the text for designated words. They make use of context clues and practice tracking the text accurately in **Cloze the Gap.**

Comprehension activities are a part of every school's reading curriculum. Understanding a text is difficult enough for beginning readers who are native speakers of English. ELL students must contend with unfamiliar vocabulary as they attempt to extract meaning from sentences, stories, and books. The texts encountered by these learners are filled with cultural and linguistic nuance, requiring a depth of understanding that will often take them years to acquire. **Predict and Check** is an exercise in which children predict words that will make up a given text based on information gleaned from previewing the title, pictures, headings, and captions. Teaching readers to ask questions as they read is a commonly used strategy, and it is especially effective with ELL students. **Spin a Question** motivates students to compose questions that can be answered by reading the text. Another question-and-answer activity that keeps students engaged is **Jeopardy,** modeled after the popular television game show. The use of **Story Maps** requires beginning readers to look at the organization of a story or book to comprehend more than just the words that make up the text.

To achieve fluency, students are often encouraged to reread familiar stories and books. **Read for Stickers** motivates children to practice reproducible or student-created mini-books many times before taking them home to share with families.

Sentence Scrambles

Number of Participants: Unlimited
Materials Needed:

- Sentence strips

- Business-sized envelopes (optional)

Brainstorm sentences around a current content theme. Write each sentence on a sentence strip. (This can be done with students or prepared ahead of time.) Place the sentences in a pocket chart, on the floor, or on a table. If appropriate, have the students work together to arrange the sentences in sequence. Read the sentences aloud in and out of sequence, asking students to listen and identify the sentence they have heard. Students then practice the sentences aloud through choral, paired, or individual reading.

After the students are familiar with the sentences, give each student a sentence strip and tell him to cut the sentence apart between words. Scramble the words and ask him to reassemble the sentence in the correct order. Give two hints: the first word will start with a capital letter, and the last word will be followed by a punctuation mark. Ask each student to read his sentence. If it is not in the right order, say the sentence aloud and have him try again after hearing the prompt. When a student successfully arranges his sentence and reads it, he mixes the words, puts them in an envelope (or just fastens them together with a paper clip) and exchanges envelopes with another student.

Continue in this way until all students have arranged several sentences.

Variations

- This activity can be easy or challenging. Easy sentences follow a repeated pattern. More difficult sentences are unrelated in structure.

- Arrange the cut-apart sentences on a pocket chart. In each sentence, turn one word face down. Ask students to identify the word on the other side. This cloze activity can be done orally, on dry erase boards, or on paper.

- Number the envelopes containing the cut-apart sentences. Have students number their papers, take words out of an envelope, and write the sentence in the correct order next to the corresponding number on their paper.

- Empty all the envelopes and gather the mixed-up words together. Use as flash cards.

Extension

- Sets of scrambled sentences make good independent learning center activities for independent or small-group work. Students arrange the words and copy them in correct order in a notebook or on a piece of paper.

Sample Lesson: Sentence Scrambles

Level: Newcomer
Objectives: To practice vocabulary related to months and family; match names and possessive pronouns; sequence months of the year; develop awareness of English syntax; and recognize sight words.
Directions: Complete some or all of the following activities.

Part One

1) Give each student a copy of the sentences about the months of the year. (Sample sentences follow this activity.) 2) Brainstorm with students in the class to fill in their names in the blanks. 3) Working together, determine whether to write "his" or "her" as the possessive pronoun. 4) Have students read sentences, using a strategy appropriate to their level. 5) Ask them to cut sentences apart on the dotted line and mix them up. 6) Direct students to sequence the sentences, working with a partner or independently. 7) Store sentence strips in envelopes for future use at a center.

Part Two

1) Ask students to remove one sentence at a time from the envelope. 2) Direct them to cut apart the words in the sentence and mix them up. 3) Working with a partner or independently, students rearrange the sentence in the correct order. The capital letter in the first word and ending punctuation will provide clues. 4) Continue cutting apart and rearranging sentences until all the words have been cut. 5) Students can turn over one random word from each sentence and ask a partner to identify the missing word. 6) Use single words as flashcards to practice with each other. 7) Return all words to the envelope.

Part Three

1) Have students use the individual words from their envelopes to create new sentences. 2) Copy the new sentences and share with the group.

SENTENCE SCRAMBLES

In January _____ can make a snowman with ___ family.

- -

In February _____ can make valentines with ___ brother.

- -

In March _____ can fly kites with __ grandpa.

- -

In April _____ can ride bikes with ___ mom.

- -

In May _____ can plant flowers with ___ sister.

- -

In June _____ can play soccer with ___ friends.

- -

In July _____ can swim with ___ cousins.

- -

In August _____ can visit the zoo with ___ aunt.

- -

In September _____ can read books with ___ teacher.

- -

In October _____ can rake leaves with ___ dad.

- -

In November _____ can play video games with ___ uncle.

- -

In December _____ can make cookies with ___ grandma.

From *Classroom Strategies: A Tool Kit for Teaching English Language Learners* by Barbara Muchisky.
Westport, CT: Teacher Ideas Press. Copyright © 2007 by Barbara Muchisky.

Find It Fast

Number of Participants: Reading group
Materials Needed:

• Reading and/or picture books

This is another activity that works well for a group of students of varying language and reading levels. Read the book or story using strategies appropriate to the group (read aloud, choral reading, guided reading, or independent reading). Tell the students to turn back to the beginning of the story. You will be asking them to find something (a picture, a word, or a sentence) on each page and point to it as quickly as they can. For example, on the first page you might say, "Point to a word that rhymes with cat." The students point to the word "sat" on the page. Now call on one student to read the word he is pointing to. Continue with the next page. For example, you might ask students to point to a word that is the opposite of "in." The children point to the word "out" in the text. Continue through the story in this fashion, asking students to find something on each page. This will give them practice in scanning for information as well as identifying words by their usage or structure. The teacher can also tailor the request to the ability of the student whose turn it will be. Less proficient students can find easier words or pictures. ("Point to the cat in the picture.") More advanced language learners can be asked to find more challenging items. ("Point to a sentence that is written in the past tense.") Maintain a quick pace to keep students focused.

Variations

Use a variety of descriptors, selecting the most appropriate for the levels of the group members:

• Initial consonants or blends

• Vowel sounds (for example, "long a," "silent e")

• Categorical words (color, month, animal, etc.)

• Singular or plural words

• Words identifying an item in the picture

• Rhyming words

• Opposites

• Parts of speech

• Verb tenses

• Words with prefixes or suffixes

• Quotations

Cloze the Gap

Number of Participants: Reading group
Materials Needed:

- Reading books

This can be an effective strategy for a group of beginning readers, not all of whom will be at the same level of English proficiency or reading ability. Students read (or follow along) silently while the teacher reads aloud. It will be helpful for most students if they point to the words as they hear the teacher read them. To teach this activity, tell students you are going to read along, then stop. When you stop, tell the group to read the next word aloud. Remind them to read only one word. Then you will continue to read along, stopping occasionally at words most students know and can read aloud. After practicing this activity as a group, tell students that now they will be taking turns in the order in which they are seated. This time when you stop, only one student will respond by reading the next word aloud. Emphasize that all students must be alert and ready for their turn by following the text closely. Now the teacher can tailor the oral cloze to the reading and English level of each child in the group. For example, if it is the turn of a newcomer or very young student, the teacher might stop at a word like "is" or "the." If it is the turn of a more advanced student, the teacher can stop at a more challenging word. Continue in this manner until the story is finished. Listening and following silently will become easier with practice. One objective of this exercise is, of course, for students to read words at their own language and reading level. More important, however, students will gain awareness of the one-to-one correspondence between the words they hear and the words they see in the printed text. It will be important to move along fairly quickly with the reading so that fluency and meaning are not lost.

Extension

- A written cloze of a text can be completed in pairs or small groups so that more proficient readers can help those who are less proficient. For beginning or intermediate level students, it is helpful to provide a word bank from which they can select the correct answers. More advanced students can complete a cloze exercise without a word bank.

Predict and Check

Number of Participants: Reading group
Materials:

• Reading books with pictures

• Chalkboard or whiteboard

This is a good activity for a short book or story. Pass out books and tell students to look at the pictures only. Give them a time limit. After they have briefly looked at all the pictures, direct them to close their books and tell you some words they predict will be found in the story. Call on students one at a time for their suggestions, writing each word on the board. Continue until there are a good number of words on the board. Now have students read the story, looking for words that have been predicted. When a student finds a word that has been written on the board, she points to the word in the book and calls out the page number where the word was found. The teacher writes the page number next to that word on the board. The search continues until no more words can be found. Circle the words that have a page number next to them and total the number of words found. Then total the number of words that have not been found and erase these words.

Note: As students catch on to this activity, they will begin to predict high-frequency words that can be expected in almost any piece of writing ("the," "is," "to," and so on.)

Variations

• Using the page numbers on the board, have all students locate the words one at a time. Then call on a student to read aloud the whole sentence that contains the word. Continue until all words have been read in context.

• Practice reading the words that have been correctly predicted, using a strategy appropriate to the level of the group (echoing, choral reading, individual reading).

• Then call on a student to be the "eraser." She calls on other students one at a time to read random words from the list. As they read a word, she locates and erases that word, continuing until all words have been erased.

• For more advanced students, have them copy the list of predicted words at the same time they are written on the board. Then ask them to work independently to find as many words as possible and write the page numbers next to the words on their lists. When everyone has finished, compare results.

Extension

• At an independent learning center, give students a copy of the words they predicted from the story. Tell them to copy the sentence in which each word is found in the text or to write an original sentence using the predicted words. They can use the word wall for spelling support.

Spin a Question

Number of Participants: Reading group
Materials Needed:

- Reading books

- Spinner graphics (commercial, reproduced, or student-made)

- Pencils

- Paper clips

- Paper, dry erase boards, or Post-It notes (optional)

A favorite comprehension strategy for elementary reading teachers is encouraging students to ask questions about what they read. Children can ask questions of their teacher, their class, their partner, and/or themselves. The answer to the questions must be found in the text and identified by both the questioner and the person answering it. Using a spinner to select a "question word" ("what," "why," "did," "can," etc.) is motivating to young learners and also requires them to practice a variety of questions. Small plastic spinners with interrogatives (or with blank spaces) can be purchased commercially from teacher supply stores or catalogs. However, it is easy to reproduce a pie-shaped spinner graphic for each child (or each pair) or to have students create their own graphics. The simplest spinner can be made with a sheet of paper containing a pie-shaped graphic in the center. (Sample spinners follow this activity.) The pieces of the pie contain the "question words" appropriate for a particular group of readers. When a student is ready to compose a question, he places a paper clip in the center of the paper and then puts the point of the pencil inside one end of the paper clip. He spins the paper clip around, and when it stops, one end will be pointing to a "question word." He uses that word to formulate his question, either orally or in writing. The person who is selected to answer the question must identify the sentence in the text which contains the answer and read it aloud (or write it).

Sample Passage

"Who will help me make the bread?" said the Little Red Hen. "Not I," said the cat. "Not I," said the dog. "Not I," said the goose. "Then I will make it myself!" said the Little Red Hen.

Sample Questions and Answers

A student spins "what" and might ask, "What did the dog say?" He calls on a volunteer who reads, "Not I, said the dog."

Another student spins "who" and might ask, "Who will make the bread?" She calls on a volunteer who reads, "Then I will make it myself!" said the Little Red Hen.

Variations

- The most basic "question words" are the familiar "wh" words: who, what where, when, how, and why. These are appropriate for younger and beginning students. Intermediate and advanced students can spin for more challenging alternatives: can (could), may (might), do (did), will (would), and so on.

- Pictures on a page can be the source of questions (or answers).

- Nonfiction texts lend themselves well to this activity. The teacher might direct students to turn chapter titles and headings into questions.

- The questioning can take place orally or, when students become more proficient, in writing. Questions can be written on paper (Post-It notes work well) or on dry erase boards.

Extension

- Collect good questions from students and place them in an independent learning center along with the text.

- Use the questions to play **Jeopardy**.

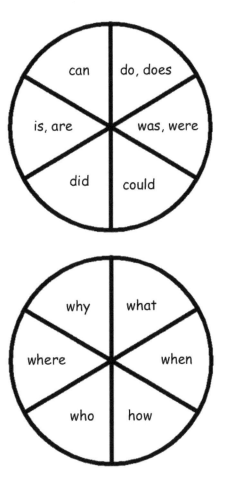

Jeopardy

Number of Participants: Unlimited
Materials Needed:

- Reading books

- Slips of paper or index cards

- Chalkboard, whiteboard, or overhead transparency

As a reading activity, Jeopardy is especially effective with nonfiction books that contain a fair amount of factual detail. After students have read a book or section of a book (using level-appropriate strategies), give them a supply of index cards or just slips of paper cut to size. Tell them they will be writing questions about what they have read to be used in a future Jeopardy game. Answers to the questions they write must be found in the text; therefore, as they write a question on a card, they must include the page number where the answer can be verified. If the book has chapter titles, headings, and picture captions, teach students how these markers can be used to formulate questions. Students can work together or independently to compose questions. The teacher may want to write questions as well to ensure that all salient questions are included in the Jeopardy game. When the questions are complete, divide them into three piles: the easiest questions are worth 100 points, the next group is worth 200 points, and the most difficult questions carry a value of 300 points. Divide the students into two groups, making sure the two groups are fairly well balanced in terms of ability. Choose a name for each team. Tell students they will not be answering as a team, but rather one student at a time. Call on the first student in one of the teams and ask her to choose a question worth 100, 200, or 300 points. When she has done so, read a question and give her 5 to 10 seconds to answer. If she answers correctly, her team receives the points, and the teacher records them on the grid. (A sample "Jeopardy grid" follows this activity.) If she answers incorrectly, or cannot answer in the allotted time, the turn passes to the first child on the other team. Play continues back and forth between the two teams. A particular question remains in play until it has been answered. When it is time for a new question, the student whose turn it is selects the point value of the question to be asked. Continue the questioning in this manner until all the questions have been answered. Total the points to determine the winning team.

Variations

- Younger or beginning students can dictate their questions to the teacher, another adult, or an advanced partner.

- When playing **Jeopardy**, it may work well for younger or less experienced readers to whisper together as a team to decide how to answer questions.

- Advanced students may be motivated by competing to answer a question. One student from each team hears the same question, and the first one to give the signal (ringing a bell, for example) tries to answer the question. If he is not correct, the other student has a chance to answer.

- Another variation for advanced students may be to mimic the television game-show format by stating the answers in the form of questions.

- Jeopardy is a good culminating activity for a thematic unit. Questions can be written by the teacher or groups of students.

Extensions

- After playing Jeopardy as a class activity, questions can be written on paper, photocopied, and put in an independent learning center along with the book. Students look up information in the book, as needed, and write answers on the paper.

- A set of jeopardy cards can be mixed randomly and placed in a center. Two (three, or four) students take turns drawing questions. If they answer correctly, they keep the card.

- It may be helpful for the teacher to write the correct answer on the back of each card ahead of time

JEOPARDY

TEAM ONE	100 POINTS	200 POINTS	300 POINTS

TEAM TWO	100 POINTS	200 POINTS	300 POINTS

Note: Use tally markers for each correct answer. Total tallies and multiply by point value to determine the final score for each team.

Story Map

Number of Participants: Unlimited
Materials Needed:

- Reading books

- Photocopied story maps

- Overhead transparency (optional)

A story map can be simple or sophisticated, depending on the students' level of English and reading proficiency. (A sample story map and a sample story pyramid follow this activity.) This type of graphic organizer is intended to help readers identify various elements of a story and its organization. Before they read a story or book (using level-appropriate strategies) introduce students to the story map. This can be done on an overhead transparency or by reviewing the photocopied map *before* beginning to read. Tell them to be thinking about this map as they are reading. After finishing the story, work together to complete the story map. Brainstorm and fill in each item on the transparency and photocopies. The section of a story map that requires students to summarize the plot is difficult, even for advanced students. The tendency is to record too many details. It may be helpful to compose the beginning and the ending before brainstorming a summary of the middle part of the story. When the story map is complete, call on students to retell the story, using the story map as a guide.

Variations

- Introduce this activity by completing a story map of a well-known fairy tale.

- Partners can use completed story maps to retell the story to each other.

- More advanced students can complete a story map independently in response to a story.

- Use blank story maps to make predictions about a story based on title, pictures, and headings.

Extension

- Story maps can be used in a reading center or in a listening center as a way to check students' comprehension.

STORY MAP

Title:_____

Author:_____

Illustrator:_____

Characters:

_____   _____

_____   _____

_____   _____

_____   _____

Setting:_____

This is what happened:

First,_____

_____

_____

Next,_____

_____

_____

Finally,_____

_____

_____

This is my opinion of this story:

_____

STORY PYRAMID

1._____

2._____ _____

3. _____ _____ _____

4. _____ _____ _____ _____

5. _____ _____ _____ _____ _____

6. _____ _____ _____ _____ _____ _____

7._____ _____ _____ _____ _____ _____ _____

Make your own story pyramid by writing:
1. The name of the main character.
2. Two words describing the main character.
3. Three words describing the setting.
4. Four words telling the problem in the story.
5. Five words telling about what happens first.
6. Six words telling about what happens in the middle.
7. Seven words telling about how the story ends.

Sample Story Pyramid

The Three Billy Goats Gruff
Troll
mean, ugly
under the bridge
goats want to cross
Troll scares first two goats
big goat knocks Troll off bridge
three goats eat grass on the hillside

Read for Stickers

Number of Participants: Unlimited
Materials Needed:

- Reproducible books (commercial, teacher-made, student-made)

- Tiny colorful stickers available in discount or teacher supply stores

A staple of the English language learning classroom is the reproducible or student-created book. These are materials that are tailored to the needs of the student and the curriculum; they are often illustrated (quite often by the students themselves) to provide a visual context or support for the text. Students can read these books to themselves, their teachers, and other students and adults in the building before taking them home to share with families. If the child has read this book aloud numerous times in school, chances are good that he will be able to do a credible job of reading when he gets home. Sight words will be reinforced, and thematic vocabulary will be memorized. Sometimes extra incentive is required for elementary-aged children to read a text many times over, and reading for stickers can be motivating. After practicing the text using strategies appropriate to the language and reading level of the students, give them each a strip of small stickers (maybe three or four stickers). Tell students these stickers are not to keep, but they may put the stickers on the book of any student who reads to *them*. In other words, the listener puts a sticker on the book of the reader. Students move around the room, reading to one another and collecting stickers. The listener can help the reader if he gets stuck on a word. Limit the time devoted to this activity by adjusting the number of stickers each child has to work with. (Note: These small stickers come in sheets that each hold perhaps 200 stickers.)

Variations

- If students have an opportunity to read for other adults in the building, they can take some stickers along to provide to the listeners. The adults may want to sign the book as well.

- Older students may prefer collecting signatures to collecting stickers.

Extension

- These books can be tape recorded by students and placed in the listening center.

Sample Lesson: Good for Today

Level: Beginner
Objective: To read and comprehend months of the year in sequence, as well as weather and clothing vocabulary.

Directions:

1) Provide a copy of *Good for Today* for each student. (A reproducible booklet follows this activity.) 2) Have children illustrate the book with items of clothing that match the text. They might do this by drawing or by cutting and pasting pictures from magazines or catalogues. Details illustrating the various weather conditions will add context to support reading. 3) Some prereading strategies might include highlighting certain words in the text. For example, all of the months could be highlighted with a light-colored marker or crayon. Weather words could be highlighted in another color, and clothing vocabulary in yet another. 4) After students have read and reread the book using strategies appropriate to their own language and reading level (choral reading, guided reading, silent reading), give each a strip of small stickers. Tell them sometimes they will be listening to someone else read, and sometimes they will be reading to another student. The listener will affix the sticker to the reader's book. Children move around the room reading to one another. 5) After they have become proficient at reading this book, encourage them to take it home to read to their families.

Variations

- A digital camera and computer might be used to make this book more personal. Students could dress to exemplify the text on each page, or even hold up a piece of clothing to illustrate the English vocabulary.

- Use **Cloze the Gap** or **Find It Fast** to practice identifying months, weather, or clothing items on each page.

Good for Today

Author: _____

January is snowy, they often say.

What clothes do you think would be good for today?

A jacket and mittens will be the best way!

February is cold, they often say.

What clothes do you think would be good for today?

Some boots and a cap will be the best way!

March is spring, they always say.

What clothes do you think would be good for today?

Some pants and a sweat shirt will be the best way!

April is rainy, they often say.

What clothes do you think would be good for today?

An umbrella and raincoat will be the best way!

May is warm, they often say.

What clothes do you think would be good for today?

Some shorts or a skirt will be the best way!

June is summer, they always say.

What clothes do you think would be good for today?

A blouse or a T-shirt will be the best way!

July is sunny, they often say.

What clothes do you think would be good for today?

A swimsuit and hat will be the best way!

August is hot, they often say.

What clothes do you think would be good for today?

A dress or some sandals will be the best way!

September is fall, they always say,

What clothes do you think would be good for today?

Some jeans and a shirt will be the best way!

October is cool, they often say.

What clothes do you think would be good for today?

Some socks and some shoes will be the best way!

November is windy, they often say.

What clothes do you think would be good for today?

A scarf and a sweater will be the best way!

December is winter, they always say.

What clothes do you think would be good for today?

A coat and some gloves will be the best way!

Chapter Five

Writing

The four domains of language acquisition, listening, speaking, and reading and writing can and should be taught simultaneously. Students do not need to know how to speak or read to begin writing. The structure of an ELL writing program will, of course, depend on the age and language levels of the children in the classroom. Another consideration will be the students' levels of first language literacy. Will it be necessary to begin with the formation of letters, or will it be possible to begin composing sentences and paragraphs?

The activities in this chapter are intended to complement a complete writing program that is designed around the students' needs and abilities. They can be adapted to fit young children and beginning students, or they can be adjusted for more advanced learners. **Brainstorming with Graphic Organizers** will facilitate the writing process for students of all ages and abilities. This type of semantic mapping will help students focus, organize, and elaborate on their ideas before beginning to write. It is especially important for younger and beginning students who don't appreciate how much they already know or what they might have to say about a topic.

Elementary students will be taught to write for many purposes. They will write lists, letters, essays, reports, and stories. Several activities are especially suited to ELL classrooms, which, by nature, usually include a wide range of developmental and language abilities among the students. Writing **Patterned Sentences,** although often considered a strategy for teaching English syntax and conventions to beginners, can also be effective in introducing more advanced students to compound and complex sentences. The great majority of ELL teachers use some form of **Journals and Logs** as components of their writing programs. It is possible to tailor these versatile tools to many areas of the curriculum, providing a frequent and regular format for writing. Frequent **Quick Writes** provide practice in responding to a writing prompt. Very often, writing assessment is accomplished in the ELL or regular education classroom by means of a personal narrative in response to a prompt. Students have a limited time to plan and execute this type of writing, so opportunities for practice are essential.

The process of **Editing** can begin when students have gained confidence in their writing and are able to produce written products with a fair amount of independence. A judicious use of editing activities will reinforce writing conventions and other aspects of effective style. A well-crafted "final product" shared with peers, adults, and family gives students a sense of pride that can motivate them to become even better writers.

Brainstorming with Graphic Organizers

Number of Participants: Unlimited
Materials Needed:

- Chalkboard or whiteboard

- Photocopied or student-made graphic organizers

- Overhead transparency (optional)

Brainstorming with graphic organizers will facilitate the writing process for ELL students. It will enable them to work more independently and keep uncertainties about spelling from blocking the flow of their ideas. There are many graphic organizers available for reproduction. Some are simple, and others are complex. It is important to remember that the purpose of a brainstorming session is to prepare for writing by recording potential content. Therefore, the simplest format that serves a particular purpose is most appropriate. In fact, two or three styles of graphic organizers should be adequate for most groups of students. When they master a format, they are more likely to be able to re-create it independently when necessary (for example, in a testing situation). Use the chalkboard or whiteboard (or overhead transparency) to brainstorm ideas and details for a writing activity. When students are just becoming familiar with a particular graphic organizer, they can fill in their own copies as the brainstorming takes place. After the brainstorming is finished, spend a few minutes of oral practice composing sentences based on the words or phrases on the graphic organizer. Make sure that students realize the difference between these words and the *sentences and paragraphs* they will be writing. As students write, some may wish to cross out items on the graphic organizer once they have been incorporated in the written text. Some children will be able to include most of the information contained in the graphic organizer, whereas others may use only a few of the ideas.

Variations

- Very young students (kindergarten and first grade) may have difficulty copying words from the board to their papers. For these students, it may be easier for the teacher to make individual photocopies of the graphic organizer that the students have helped to create in their brainstorming session.

- Younger or newcomer students with limited vocabulary may benefit from drawing and labeling pictures on their graphic organizers.

- For beginning students, it can be helpful to ask each student, "What will your first sentence be when you begin to write?" Another strategy is to compose the first sentence as a group, using the graphic organizer, and have everyone write that first sentence on their paper.

- As students become more experienced in using graphic organizers, it will not always be necessary to write the ideas on the board or overhead transparency. As the group talks about the subject matter, students can fill in their graphic organizers with greater independence.

- More advanced students can use classroom resources (books, dictionaries, pictures, or the Internet) to complete a graphic organizer.

Extensions

- Students use a graphic organizer to collect information gleaned from interviews (with family members, other students, adults in the building, or community workers) in preparation for a writing assignment.

- Challenge advanced students to create a graphic organizer for the class.

Patterned Sentences

Number of Participants: Unlimited
Materials Needed:

- Paper or journals

- Chalkboard or whiteboard

Teaching children to write patterned sentences may not appeal to those who regard this as a rote activity that does not inspire much creativity or independent thinking. However, for students who are just beginning to write in English, composing patterned sentences can give them some measure of choice and independence as they become familiar with English syntax. Patterned sentences can be simple or more complex, depending on the writing ability and language level of the students. On the chalkboard, brainstorm a web around one theme: for example, "animal legs." Ask students to name animals with two legs and write their suggestions on the board, grouped together. Then have them name animals with four legs, six legs, and no legs. Group these suggested animals loosely together on the board according to the number of legs. Now, working together, compose the first sentence that all students will write on their papers. For beginners, a sentence might be: "A bird has two legs." Then ask students *orally* to compose similar sentences about animals with two legs. After a few examples are given, tell students to write some of these sentences on their paper. They will be able to refer to the first sentence for the pattern and to the board for spelling names of other animals. While students are working independently, circulate and, when it seems that a student has mastered the first pattern, encourage him to write some sentences about animals that have four legs, six legs, or no legs. Some students will produce many sentences, and others just a few. After they have written for a time, call on students to read one or two of their sentences aloud.

Variations

- For more proficient students, set up a more complex pattern. For example, "A bird has two legs, but a spider has six legs." Or "A dog has more legs than a bird."

- Patterned sentences can be used to practice thematic vocabulary (months, colors, food, and so on).

- Patterned sentences are also effective in practicing grammatical structures. For example, "If I were a police officer, I would help keep people safe." "If I were a librarian, I would help people find books."

- More advanced students can write patterned sentences without a web on the board. They can rely on invented spelling, use dictionaries or the word wall.

- Use Venn diagrams to create patterned sentences that show comparison or contrast.

Extensions

- Place vocabulary cards in an independent learning center along with a starter sentence. Challenge students to write as many sentences as they can during center time.

- Write and illustrate mini-books using patterned sentences.

Journals and Logs

Number of Participants: Unlimited
Materials Needed:

- Notebooks

Journals and logs provide a forum for observing and recording information, ideas, and opinions. They can be a collection of writings unified around a particular purpose or theme. Or these notebooks can simply be a place to write on a regular basis for a variety of purposes to have a record of writing growth over time. Some teachers assign journal writing as an individual, private endeavor and do not read what students write in them. Others read and respond to entries but do not make any corrections. Still others use journals and logs as a vehicle for editing practice and make suggestions or corrections as well as responding to content.

Uncertainties about spelling often frustrate students and block the flow of children's writing. It is a good practice to plan ahead to minimize this concern by providing a word bank, graphic organizer, dictionaries, a word wall, or other easily used resources. If students are to use invented spelling, they usually must be taught explicitly how to do this and given an opportunity to practice.

Variations

- Keep a daily log about weather and change of seasons.

- Keep a log of observations of a class pet, science project, plants, or trees.

- Keep a **Word of the Day** Journal, writing sentences or a paragraph defining or using the word.

- Keep a math journal. Describe math processes in writing. This exercise can clarify students' thinking about mathematical concepts.

- Keep a dialogue journal. The teacher keeps up a conversation in writing with students. Every journal will take a unique direction.

- Create shorter journals or logs to accompany each thematic unit. This can become a place to enter vocabulary, information, questions, reports, or any other kind of writing associated with a given theme. Share it with families at the end of the unit.

- Keep a literature journal or log. This can be a written conversation between student and teacher about books read in class or independently. Or it can be a repository for book summaries, reports, or responses to literature.

- Older students with good keyboarding skills can write journal entries on a computer. They can share with teachers or other students via e-mail.

Quick Writes

Number of Students: Unlimited
Materials Needed:

- Writing notebooks or paper

- Chalkboard or whiteboard

Plan this activity for a short amount of time each day (5–10 minutes), every few days (10–15 minutes), or once a week (15–20 minutes). Write a prompt on the board and tell students to write as much as possible without stopping. (Sample prompts follow this activity.) A kitchen timer can help students get a sense of how long they will typically have for this assignment. You may wish to write your own responses to the prompts as a model to share with students. At first, students will probably only write one or two sentences in the short time period; however, as they become used to quick writes as a regular activity, they will begin to write longer entries. Encourage students to focus on ideas and fluency. Don't insist on correct spelling and conventions in this type of writing. Very young students or beginners may need to draw and label pictures before they are able to write sentences. If you occasionally write comments about entries in students' notebooks, focus on content rather than form.

Variations

- Students can occasionally share their writing with a partner. The teacher can also share some of the students' writing to motivate those who may be having trouble getting started.

- From time to time, ask students to choose a favorite entry to edit, revise, publish, and share with the group.

Extensions

- This makes a good independent learning center activity. One purpose of quick writes is to encourage independence. It will be necessary to have very clear expectations so that students are productive when they write without supervision.

SAMPLE PROMPTS FROM EASY TO CHALLENGING

Tell about yourself.

- -

Tell about your friends.

- -

Tell about your classroom.

- -

Tell about your school.

- -

Tell about your teachers.

- -

Tell about the best part of your day.

- -

Tell about what you will do after school today.

- -

Write about your favorite game or sport.

- -

Write about your favorite food.

- -

Write about your favorite book.

- -

Write about your favorite TV show.

- -

Write about your favorite part of school.

- -

Write about your favorite holiday.

Describe how you look.

Describe how someone in your family looks.

Describe how your teacher looks.

Describe how your best friend looks.

Describe how your house looks.

Describe how your car looks.

Tell about a time when you felt happy.

Tell about a time when you laughed a lot.

Tell about a time when you got lost (or lost something).

Tell about a time when you felt proud of yourself.

Tell about a time when you had the most fun.

Tell about a time when you helped someone.

If you could, what would you change about how you look?

If you could, what would you change about where you live?

If you could, what would you change about your school?

If you could, what would you change about the weather?

If you could, what would you change about school lunches?

If you could, what would you change about the world?

When you get older, what would you like to study or learn to do?

When you get older, what job would you like to do?

When you get older, what kind of car would you like to drive?

What would you do if you were the principal of this school?

What would you do if you were the mayor of this city?

What would you do if you were the president of the United States?

What would you do to make the world a better place to live?

Editing

Number of Participants: Unlimited
Materials Needed:

- Chalkboard or white board

- Editing graphic with symbols (optional)

- Highlighters (optional)

- Overhead transparencies (optional)

Strategies for teaching editing vary according to the age and language level of the students. Very little editing is called for in the early stages of writing in a new language. When editing symbols are introduced, be sure to use the format most commonly accepted throughout the school. (A sample editing graphic follows this activity.)

It is a good practice to start with one or two basic skills and gradually increase the complexity of the editing process. Point out correct usage as well as errors that need to be corrected. Write real, student-produced sentences on the board or overhead transparency, making sure to include at least one sentence from every student's writing. There is no need to identify the authors of the sentences; just make sure students know that everyone's writing is represented. Give students a copy of these sentences. Choose one or two items as a focal point for a given lesson. If, for example, the focus is on capital letters and end punctuation, call on students to highlight the first letter at the beginning and the space at the end of the sentence. Ask if any changes are necessary. Make necessary changes, asking students to verbalize the reason for the change. When students become comfortable with recognizing errors, teach them the editing symbol for those particular errors. The next editing lesson can be similar to the first; however, have students write in the editing symbols instead of using a highlighter. Tell them to only mark the items that need changing. After comparing results, ask students to rewrite each sentence, making the correction indicated by the editing symbol. Give children a chance to practice editing their own writing regularly, gradually teaching new symbols to add to their repertoire.

It is important to avoid editing every piece of students' writing. Too much emphasis on correction may result in writing that is stale and repetitive. A certain amount of risk-taking needs to be encouraged to keep writing fresh and inventive.

Variations

- Call on students to take turns writing editing marks or rewrites on the board or overhead transparency.

- Use dry erase boards to practice editing marks. Display a sentence with one error on the board or overhead transparency. Tell students to write the appropriate editing symbol on their dry erase boards. Compare results.

Variations

- Create a graphic that reminds students of the most common editing marks used in the school. Consider laminating a copy of this graphic for students to keep in their desk, cubbie, writing folder, or another convenient place.

- Make editing a daily routine. Write a sentence that requires editing on the board every day. When students enter the room, they revise the sentence on a paper or dry erase board. Or conceal an error every day in the **Daily Message**. Ask students to detect the error. Call on a volunteer to write the appropriate editing mark on the Daily Message before proceeding with that activity.

- Consider peer editing for older, more advanced students. Limit editing to one or two basic conventions. Spend a fair amount of time modeling this activity before asking students to edit a partner's writing.

- Provide colorful pens or special, decorative paper for important revisions. This will motivate students to undertake rewriting with more enthusiasm.

Extension

- Create an editing center when students become more experienced with editing symbols and revision. Keep a copy of the editing graphic at the center, along with dictionaries or other resources. You may want to give students some choice in determining which writing they want to edit and/or revise.

- Students may want to keep a copy of an editing graphic at home to use with homework assignments. Challenge them to explain the symbols to their families.

- Display student writing that has been successfully (not perfectly) edited in a prominent place.

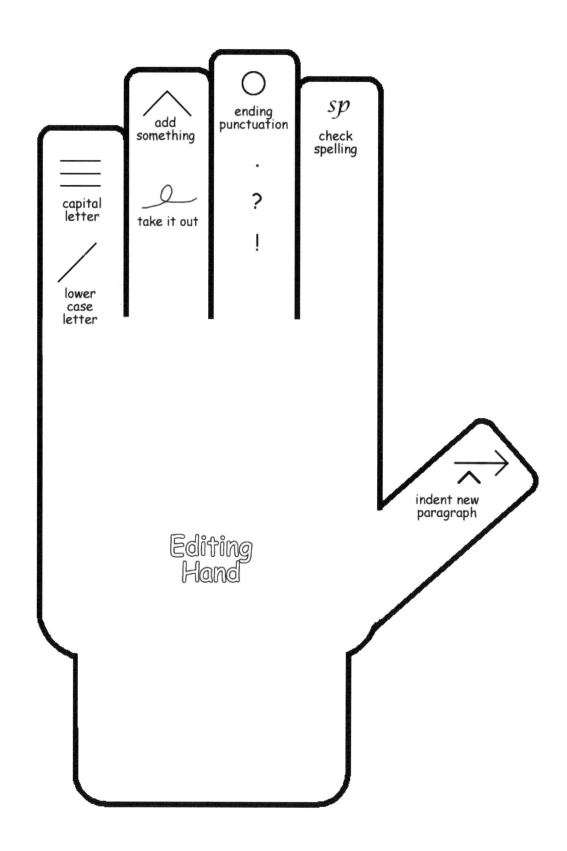

About the Author

BARBARA MUCHISKY is a retired ELL (English language learners) teacher for the Lincoln, Nebraska Public Schools. She has taught children and adult learners for more than twenty-five years.